In The 100 Best Poems of All Time,
you'll find . . .

Lines to transport you to another world . . .

"Midway upon the journey of our life
I found myself within a forest dark . . ."
—*from* "Inferno" *by Dante Alighieri*

Expressions of passionate love . . .

"If I meet
you suddenly, I can't
speak—my tongue is broken;
a thin flame runs under
my skin . . ."
—*from* "He is a God in My Eyes" *by Sappho*

Words that voice our innermost feelings . . .

"Where is Echo, beheld of no man,
Only heard on river and mere,—
She whose beauty was more than human?
But where are the snows of yester-year? . . ."
—*from* "The Ballad of Ladies of the Past"
by François Villon

more . . .

Poems of beauty and bravery . . .

"She walks in beauty, like the night
Of cloudless climes and starry skies . . ."
—*from* "She Walks in Beauty" *by Lord Byron*

Words to touch and challenge you . . .

"What happens to a dream deferred?
Does it dry up
like a raisin in the sun? . . ."
—*from* "Harlem [Dream Deferred]" *by Langston Hughes*

And verses that will make you smile . . .

"It looked extremely rocky for the Mudville Nine
that day;
The score stood two to four, with but an inning
left to play . . ."
—*from* "Casey at the Bat" *by Ernest Thayer*

THE 100 BEST POEMS OF ALL TIME

EDITED BY

LESLIE POCKELL

WARNER BOOKS

NEW YORK   BOSTON

Copyright information continued on page 187.

Warner Books

Time Warner Book Group
1271 Avenue of the Americas, New York, NY 10020
Visit our Web site at www.twbookmark.com

Printed in the United States of America
First Edition: March 2001
Special Sales Edition: July 2005
10 9 8 7 6 5 4 3 2 1

The Library of Congress has cataloged the first edition as follows:
    The 100 best poems of all time / edited by Leslie Pockell.
        p. cm.
    Includes index.
    ISBN 0-446-67681-0
        1. Poetry—Collections. 2. Poetry—Translations into English.
    I. Title: One hundred best poems of all time. II. Pockell, Leslie.

PN6101 .A16 2001
808.81—dc21

00-060014

Book design and text composition by Ellen Gleeson

ISBN: 0-446-57907-6 (Special Sales Edition)

Contents

Introduction

I know, I know, it probably seems outrageously arrogant to declare that we, whoever "we" are, have selected the hundred best poems of all time and placed them in this little volume. Who are we to decide what is best among the countless poetic works of all cultures and all times? Well, at least we attracted your attention. But naming anthologies appropriately is not easy. In 1861 Francis Palgrave called his landmark volume *The Golden Treasury*, whatever that means, and there have been many treasuries and collections of one person or another's "favorite" poems ever since. Usually, though, inclusion is based on no better criterion than the collector's own taste or opinion, or that of some other, similarly subjective, authority (Palgrave asked Tennyson for his input). Given the principles on which it was assembled, we feel that this present collection has as much credibility as many other lists of the best and the greatest that have circulated during the recent turn of the century.

Our primary objective in assembling these poems was to provide a small, easily portable volume that would contain the essential works that most readers would expect to find in a book of the best poems, along with some less familiar but equally gratifying selections. To maximize the breadth of the collection, while maintaining a convenient format suitable for browsing through or dipping into at any odd moment, whatever one's mood, we decided to include no more than one poem per poet, in the manner of the thirteenth-century Japanese collection *Hyakunin Isshu* (one hundred men, one work). The poems are arranged in a roughly chronological order (based on the poets' birth dates), from the ninth century B.C.E. to the late twentieth century, and represent virtually every major language group. (Many of the poems appear in English translations by poets with major reputations in their own right.) Most poems included are complete, but several are excerpts from larger works. Some are examples of high art; others exemplify popular culture (we have taken as a byword Stephen Spender's observation that those who try to put poetry on a pedestal only succeed in putting it on the shelf). We have also inclined toward poetry that is best appreciated when recited or read aloud (accounting for the relatively large proportion of lyrical poems to be found here); we hold with W. H. Auden that the best definition of poetry is "memorable speech."

We hope that everyone who reads this book will find it an enjoyable and at times inspiring (or consoling) companion. That some readers may disagree with our assessment of the one hundred best poems of all time shouldn't prevent them or others from enjoying these poems on their own considerable merits, and of course those readers objecting to the selection are free to compile their own anthologies.

This book would not have been possible without the early and enthusiastic support of Maureen Egen and Jamie Raab. Shannon Beatty, Vicki Bott, Amy Einhorn, Jennifer Landers, and Karen Melnyk provided essential editorial contributions.

From The Iliad

HOMER
(9TH–8TH CENTURY B.C.E.?)

This version of Homer's great epic of wounded honor and vengeance was translated into English by George Chapman (1559?–1634), a contemporary of both Shakespeare and John Donne.

Achilles' banefull wrath resound, O Goddesse, that
    imposd
Infinite sorrowes on the Greekes, and many brave
    soules losd
From breasts Heroique—sent them farre, to that
    invisible cave
That no light comforts; and their lims to dogs and
    vultures gave.
To all which Jove's will gave effect; from whom
    first strife begunne
Betwixt Atrides, king of men, and Thetis' godlike
    Sonne.

He Is More Than a Hero

SAPPHO
(7TH CENTURY B.C.E.)

Only fragments remain of the lyrical work of this legendary poet, many of them poems of friendship and love of other women.

He is a god in my eyes—
the man who is allowed
to sit beside you—he

who listens intimately
to the sweet murmur of
your voice, the enticing

laughter that makes my own
heart beat fast. If I meet
you suddenly, I can't

speak—my tongue is broken;
a thin flame runs under
my skin; seeing nothing,

hearing only my own ears
drumming, I drip with sweat;
trembling shakes my body

and I turn paler than
dry grass. At such times
death isn't far from me.

Psalm 23

THE PSALMIST
(6TH CENTURY B.C.E.?)

While the original Hebrew text of the twenty-third Psalm is usually ascribed to the biblical King David, this familiar English rendition is that of the King James Version of the Old Testament. The translation was the work of scholars who were contemporaries of Shakespeare, and almost his equal in the expressiveness and beauty of their language.

The LORD is my shepherd; I shall not want.
He maketh me to lie down in green pastures: he leadeth
    me beside the still waters.
He restoreth my soul: he leadeth me in the paths of
    righteousness for his name's sake.
Yea, though I walk through the valley of the shadow of
    death, I will fear no evil: for thou art with me;
    thy rod and thy staff they comfort me.
Thou preparest a table before me in the presence of mine
    enemies: thou anointest my head with oil;
    my cup runneth over.
Surely goodness and mercy shall follow me all the days of
    my life: and I will dwell in the house of the LORD
    for ever.

From The Song of Songs
[Chapter One]

ANONYMOUS
(3RD CENTURY B.C.E.)

Though the lyrics in this biblical work have been attributed to King Solomon, they were collected in their present form as late as the third century B.C.E. Whether they are read as allegorical songs of passionate adoration of God, or frank expressions of human love, their beauty and power in the King James translation are undeniable.

—〰—

The song of songs, which is Solomon's.
Let him kiss me with the kisses of his mouth: for thy love
    is better than wine.
Because of the savour of thy good ointments thy name is
    as ointment poured forth, therefore do the virgins
    love thee.
Draw me, we will run after thee: the king hath brought me
    into his chambers: we will be glad and rejoice in
    thee, we will remember thy love more than wine:
    the upright love thee.
I am black, but comely, O ye daughters of Jerusalem, as
    the tents of Kedar, as the curtains of Solomon.
Look not upon me, because I am black, because the sun
    hath looked upon me: my mother's children were
    angry with me; they made me the keeper of the
    vineyards; but mine own vineyard have I not kept.
Tell me, O thou whom my soul loveth, where thou feedest,
    where thou makest thy flock to rest at noon: for
    why should I be as one that turneth aside by the
    flocks of thy companions?
If thou know not, O thou fairest among women, go thy
    way forth by the footsteps of the flock, and feed thy
    kids beside the shepherds' tents.

I have compared thee, O my love, to a company of horses
in Pharaoh's chariots.
Thy cheeks are comely with rows of jewels, thy neck with
chains of gold.
We will make thee borders of gold with studs of silver.
While the king sitteth at his table, my spikenard sendeth
forth the smell thereof.
A bundle of myrrh is my wellbeloved unto me; he shall lie
all night betwixt my breasts.
My beloved is unto me as a cluster of camphire in the
vineyards of En-gedi.
Behold, thou art fair, my love; behold, thou art fair; thou
hast doves' eyes.
Behold, thou art fair, my beloved, yea, pleasant: also our
bed is green.
The beams of our house are cedar, and our rafters of fir.

Song 5 to Lesbia

CATULLUS [GAIUS VALERIUS CATULLUS]
(84–54 B.C.E.)

In his brief life Catullus built a reputation for communicating passion with wit and lyricism that has been sustained in every era to the present day. The following translation is by the early seventeenth-century English poet Richard Crashaw.

Come and let us live my Deare,
Let us love and never feare,
What the sourest Fathers say:
Brightest *Sol* that dyes to day
Lives againe as blith to morrow,
But if we darke sons of sorrow
Set; O then, how long a Night
Shuts the Eyes of our short light!
Then let amorous kisses dwell
On our lips, begin and tell
A Thousand, and a Hundred score
An Hundred, and a Thousand more,
Till another Thousand smother
That, and that wipe off another.
Thus at last when we have numbered
Many a Thousand, many a Hundred;
We'll confound the reckoning quite,
And lose our selves in wild delight:
While our joyes so multiply,
As shall mocke the envious eye.

From The Aeneid

VIRGIL [PUBLIUS VERGILIUS MARO]
(70–19 B.C.E.)

Clearly influenced by Homer's example, Virgil's epic tells of how the brave Aeneas sailed from the shores of ruined Troy to found the settlement that would become Rome. This version is by the English poet John Dryden (1631–1700).

Arms, and the Man I sing, who, forc'd by Fate,
And haughty Juno's unrelenting Hate;
Expell'd and exil'd, left the Trojan Shoar:
Long Labours, both by Sea and Land he bore;
And in the doubtful War, before he won
The Latian Realm, and built the destin'd Town:
His banish'd Gods restor'd to Rites Divine,
And setl'd sure Succession in his Line:
From whence the Race of Alban Fathers come,
And the long Glories of Majestick Rome.
O Muse! the Causes and the Crimes relate,
What Goddess was provok'd, and whence her hate:
For what Offence the Queen of Heav'n began
To persecute so brave, so just a Man!
Involv'd his anxious Life in endless Cares,
Expos'd to Wants, and hurry'd into Wars!
Can Heav'nly Minds such high resentment show;
Or exercise their Spight in Human Woe?

From *Metamorphoses*

OVID [PUBLIUS OVIDIUS NASO]
(43 B.C.E.–17 C.E.)

This collection of myths of transformations itself transforms uncon-
nected stories into a brilliant verse narrative that has influenced
poets and artists for many centuries. The excerpt below relates the
story of how the world was created. The translation is by John
Dryden.

Of bodies chang'd to various forms, I sing:
Ye Gods, from whom these miracles did spring,
Inspire my numbers with celestial heat;
Till I my long laborious work compleat:
And add perpetual tenour to my rhimes,
Deduc'd from Nature's birth, to Caesar's times.
Before the seas, and this terrestrial ball,
And Heav'n's high canopy, that covers all,
Once was the face of Nature; if a face:
Rather a rude and indigested mass:
A lifeless lump, unfashion'd, and unfram'd,
Of jarring seeds; and justly Chaos nam'd.
No sun was lighted up, the world to view;
No moon did yet her blunted horns renew:
Nor yet was Earth suspended in the sky,
Nor pois'd, did on her own foundations lye:
Nor seas about the shores their arms had thrown;
But earth, and air, and water, were in one.
Thus air was void of light, and earth unstable,
And water's dark abyss unnavigable.
No certain form on any was imprest;
All were confus'd, and each disturb'd the rest.
For hot and cold were in one body fixt;
And soft with hard, and light with heavy mixt.

8

Drinking Alone in the Moonlight

LI PO
(701–762)

The first of three great poets who flourished during China's T'ang Dynasty (618–907), Li Po was famous for his romantic poems of escape from reality through imaginary voyages or wine drinking. He is traditionally supposed to have drowned while attempting to embrace the moon's reflection in the water.

—⟋⟍—

Beneath the blossoms with a pot of wine,
No friends at hand, so I poured alone;
I raised my cup to invite the moon,
Turned to my shadow, and we became three.
Now the moon had never learned about drinking,
And my shadow had merely followed my form,
But I quickly made friends with the moon and my shadow;
To find pleasure in life, make the most of the spring.

Whenever I sang, the moon swayed with me;
Whenever I danced, my shadow went wild.
Drinking, we shared our enjoyment together;
Drunk, then each went off on his own.
But forever agreed on dispassionate revels,
We promised to meet in the far Milky Way.

Moonlit Night

TU FU
(712–770)

Generally recognized as the greatest of all Chinese poets, Tu Fu lived a life filled with hardship, which perhaps influenced the humanity and compassion that informs his best work. This poem was translated by the modern Indian poet and novelist Vikram Seth.

In Fuzhou, far away, my wife is watching
The moon alone tonight, and my thoughts fill
With sadness for my children, who can't think
Of me here in Changan; they're too young still.
Her cloud-soft hair is moist with fragrant mist.
In the clear light her white arms sense the chill.
When will we feel the moonlight dry our tears,
Leaning together on our windowsill?

Madly Singing in the Mountains

PO CHU-I
(772–846)

A successful civil servant, Po was briefly exiled in his early forties. This poem, which alludes to his exile, was translated by the great British Asian scholar Arthur Waley, who introduced many of the greatest figures of Chinese and Japanese literature to the English-speaking world.

There is no one among men that has not a special failing:
And my failing consists in writing verses.
I have broken away from the thousand ties of life:
But this infirmity still remains behind.
Each time that I look at a fine landscape:
Each time that I meet a loved friend,
I raise my voice and recite a stanza of poetry
And am glad as though a god had crossed my path.
Ever since the day I was banished to Hsün-yang
Half my time I have lived among the hills.
And often, when I have finished a new poem,
Alone I climb the road to the Eastern Rock.
I lean my body on the banks of white stone:
I pull down with my hands a green cassia branch.
My mad singing startles the valleys and hills:
The apes and birds all come to peep.
Fearing to become a laughingstock to the world,
I choose a place that is unfrequented by men.

Rubaiyat 51

OMAR KHAYYAM
(1048–1131)

A Persian mathematician and astronomer as well as a poet, Omar was the putative author of the collection of short philosophical poems known as the Rubaiyat *(the word means "quatrains"). Edward FitzGerald, using two different manuscripts, assembled and adapted the separate poems into a single work, published in 1859.*

The Moving Finger writes; and, having writ,
Moves on: nor all thy Piety nor Wit
Shall lure it back to cancel half a Line,
Nor all thy Tears wash out a Word of it.

From Inferno

DANTE ALIGHIERI
(1265–1321)

One of the foundation works of world literature, Dante's Divine
Comedy—*composed of* Inferno, Purgatorio, *and* Paradiso—*blends
religious allegory, political and social commentary, and medieval
philosophy into a powerful symphonic poem. In the following
excerpt from Canto I—translated here by the American poet Henry
Wadsworth Longfellow—Dante encounters his mentor, the Roman
poet Virgil, who will serve as his guide to the Underworld.*

MIDWAY upon the journey of our life
I found myself within a forest dark,
For the straightforward pathway had been lost.

Ah me! how hard a thing it is to say
What was this forest savage, rough, and stern,
Which in the very thought renews the fear.

So bitter is it, death is little more;
But of the good to treat, which there I found,
Speak will I of the other things I saw there.

I cannot well repeat how there I entered,
So full was I of slumber at the moment
In which I had abandoned the true way.

But after I had reached a mountain's foot,
At that point where the valley terminated,
Which had with consternation pierced my heart,

Upward I looked, and I beheld its shoulders
Vested already with that planet's rays
Which leadeth others right by every road.

Then was the fear a little quieted
That in my heart's lake had endured throughout
The night, which I had passed so piteously

And even as he, who, with distressful breath,
Forth issued from the sea upon the shore,
Turns to the water perilous and gazes;

So did my soul, that still was fleeing onward,
Turn itself back to re-behold the pass
Which never yet a living person left.

After my weary body I had rested,
The way resumed I on the desert slope,
So that the firm foot ever was the lower.

And lo! almost where the ascent began,
A panther light and swift exceedingly,
Which with a spotted skin was covered o'er!

And never moved she from before my face,
Nay, rather did impede so much my way,
That many times I to return had turned.

The time was the beginning of the morning,
And up the sun was mounting with those stars
That with him were, what time the Love Divine

At first in motion set those beauteous things;
So were to me occasion of good hope,
The variegated skin of that wild beast,

The hour of time, and the delicious season;
But not so much, that did not give me fear
A lion's aspect which appeared to me.

He seemed as if against me he were coming
With head uplifted, and with ravenous hunger,
So that it seemed the air was afraid of him;

And a she-wolf, that with all hungerings
Seemed to be laden in her meagreness,
And many folk has caused to live forlorn!

She brought upon me so much heaviness,
With the affright that from her aspect came,
That I the hope relinquished of the height.

And as he is who willingly acquires,
And the time comes that causes him to lose,
Who weeps in all his thoughts and is despondent,

E'en such made me that beast withouten peace,
Which, coming on against me by degrees
Thrust me back thither where the sun is silent

While I was rushing downward to the lowland,
Before mine eyes did one present himself,
Who seemed from long-continued silence hoarse.

When I beheld him in the desert vast,
"Have pity on me," unto him I cried,
"Whiche'er thou art, or shade or real man!"

He answered me: "Not man; man once I was,
And both my parents were of Lombardy,
And Mantuans by country both of them.

Sub Julio was I born, though it was late,
And lived at Rome under the good Augustus,
During the time of false and lying gods.

A poet was I, and I sang that just
Son of Anchises, who came forth from Troy,
After that Ilion the superb was burned

But thou, why goest thou back to such annoyance?
Why climb'st thou not the Mount Delectable
Which is the source and cause of every joy?"

"Now, art thou that Virgilius and that fountain
Which spreads abroad so wide a river of speech?"
I made response to him with bashful forehead.

"O, of the other poets honor and light,
Avail me the long study and great love
That have impelled me to explore thy volume!

Thou art my master, and my author thou,
Thou art alone the one from whom I took
The beautiful style that has done honour to me."

Remembrance

PETRARCH [FRANCESCO PETRARCA]
(1304–1374)

Petrarch's poetry—its lyricism, language, and form—has had an enduring influence on the Western tradition. The poem is a translation by the Elizabethan poet Thomas Wyatt, one of the first to introduce Petrarch to English readers.

—⁓—

They flee from me, that sometime me did seek
    With naked foot, stalking in my chamber.
I have seen them gentle, tame and meek,
    That now are wild, and do not remember
    That sometime they put themselves in danger
        To take bread at my hand; and now they range
        Busily seeking with a continual change.

Thanked be fortune it hath been otherwise
    Twenty times better; but once, in special,
In thin array, after a pleasant guise,
    When her loose gown from her shoulders did fall,
    And she me caught in her arms long and small,
        There with all sweetly did me kiss
        And softly said, "Dear heart, how like you this?"

It was no dream; I lay broad waking:
    But all is turned, thorough my gentleness,
Into a strange fashion of forsaking;
    And I have leave to go of her goodness,
    And she also to use newfangleness.
        But since that I so kindly am served,
        I would fain know what she hath deserved.

From The General Prologue to
The Canterbury Tales

GEOFFREY CHAUCER
(1340–1400)

Although, like all this great poet's work, The Canterbury Tales *is written in Middle English, its power and beauty, as well as its meaning, are easily understood when it is read aloud.*

Whan that Aprille, with hise shoures soote,
The droghte of March hath perced to the roote
And bathed every veyne in swich licour,
Of which vertu engendred is the flour;
Whan Zephirus eek with his swete breeth
Inspired hath in every holt and heeth
The tendre croppes, and the yonge sonne
Hath in the Ram his halfe cours yronne,
And smale foweles maken melodye,
That slepen al the nyght with open eye—
So priketh hem Nature in hir corages—
Thanne longen folk to goon on pilgrimages
And palmeres for to seken straunge strondes
To ferne halwes, kowthe in sondry londes;
And specially, from every shires ende
Of Engelond, to Caunturbury they wende,
The hooly blisful martir for to seke
That hem hath holpen, whan that they were seeke.

The Ballad of Ladies of the Past

FRANÇOIS VILLON
(1431–1463?)

At once a scholar, a thief, and a brilliantly lyrical writer, Villon has been called the father of French poetry. This version of his most famous work is by the English Pre-Raphaelite poet and artist Dante Gabriel Rossetti.

—ɯ—

Tell me now in what hidden way is
    Lady Flora the lovely Roman?
Where's Hipparchia, and where is Thais,
    Neither of them the fairer woman?
    Where is Echo, beheld of no man,
Only heard on river and mere,—
    She whose beauty was more than human? . . .
But where are the snows of yester-year?

Where's Heloise, the learned nun,
    For whose sake Abeillard, I ween,
Lost manhood and put priesthood on?
    (From Love he won such dule and teen!)
    And where, I pray you, is the Queen
Who willed that Buridan should steer
    Sewed in a sack's mouth down the Seine? . . .
But where are the snows of yester-year?

White Queen Blanche, like a queen of lilies,
    With a voice like any mermaiden—
Bertha Broadfoot, Beatrice, Alice,
    And Ermengarde the lady of Maine,—
    And that good Joan whom Englishmen
At Rouen doomed and burned her there,—
    Mother of God, where are they then? . . .
But where are the snows of yester-year?

19

Sonnet 18

WILLIAM SHAKESPEARE
(1564–1616)

This is perhaps the most familiar of Shakespeare's 154 published sonnets, especially for its immortal first line. The entire poem is an eloquent appreciation of the transient nature of life and beauty, and a tribute to the power of art.

—m—

Shall I compare thee to a summer's day?
Thou art more lovely and more temperate:
Rough winds do shake the darling buds of May,
And summer's lease hath all too short a date:
Sometime too hot the eye of heaven shines,
And often is his gold complexion dimmed;
And every fair from fair sometimes declines,
By chance, or nature's changing course untrimmed;
But thy eternal summer shall not fade,
Nor lose possession of that fair thou owest;
Nor shall Death brag thou wanderest in his shade
When in eternal lines to time thou growest:
So long as men can breathe, or eyes can see,
So long lives this, and this gives life to thee.

Go and Catch a Falling Star

JOHN DONNE
(1572–1631)

Despite Donne's religious calling (he was dean of St. Paul's Cathedral in London), his poetry is notable for its eroticism and sometimes cynical worldview, as well as for its striking imagery.

Go and catch a falling star,
    Get with child a mandrake root,
Tell me where all past years are,
    Or who cleft the devil's foot,
Teach me to hear mermaids singing,
Or to keep off envy's stinging,
        And find
        What wind
Serves to advance an honest mind.

If thou be'st born to strange sights,
    Things invisible to see,
Ride ten thousand days and nights,
    Till age snow white hairs on thee,
Thou, when thou return'st, wilt tell me,
All strange wonders that befell thee,
        And swear,
        No where
Lives a woman true, and fair.

If thou find'st one, let me know,
    Such a pilgrimage were sweet;
Yet do not, I would not go,
    Though at next door we might meet;

Though she were true, when you met her,
And last, till you write your letter,
      Yet she
      Will be
False, ere I come, to two, or three.

Song to Celia II

BEN JONSON
(1572–1637)

*A contemporary and friend of Shakespeare, Jonson is remembered
primarily as a playwright, but this familiar romantic lyric may be his
most popular work.*

—〰—

Drink to me only with thine eyes,
And I will pledge with mine;
Or leave a kiss but in the cup,
And I'll not look for wine.

The thirst that from the soul doth rise
Doth ask a drink divine;
But might I of Jove's nectar sup,
I would not change for thine.

I sent thee late a rosy wreath,
No so much honoring thee,
As giving it a hope that there
It could not withered be.

But thou thereon didst only breathe,
And sent'st it back to me,
Since when it grows and smells, I swear,
Not of itself but thee.

To the Virgins, to Make Much of Time

ROBERT HERRICK
(1591–1674)

This lyrical tribute to youth is reminiscent of the work of Herrick's greatest influence, Ben Jonson.

Gather ye rosebuds while ye may,
    Old Time is still a-flying:
And this same flower that smiles today
    Tomorrow will be dying.

The glorious lamp of heaven, the Sun,
    The higher he's a-getting
The sooner will his race be run,
    And nearer he's to setting.

That age is best which is the first,
    When youth and blood are warmer;
But being spent, the worse, and worst
    Times, still succeed the former.

Then be not coy, but use your time;
    And while ye may, go marry:
For having lost but once your prime,
    You may forever tarry.

Jordan

GEORGE HERBERT
(1593–1633)

This apparently simple poem, ostensibly the poet's own quarrel with poetic convention, reveals additional layers of meaning and beauty with every rereading. (It's worth remembering that the Jordan River separated the biblical Wilderness from the Promised Land.)

—ɱ—

Who sayes that fictions onely and false hair
Become a verse? Is there in truth no beautie?
Is all good structure in a winding stair?
May no lines passe, except they do their dutie
　　Not to a true, but painted chair?

Is it no verse, except enchanted groves
And sudden arbours shadow course-spunne lines?
Must purling streams refresh a lover's loves?
Must all be vail'd, while he that reads divines,
　　Catching the sense at two removes?

Shepherds are honest people; let them sing:
Riddle who list for me, and pull for Prime:
I envie no man's nightingale or spring;
Nor let them punish me with loss of rime
　　Who plainly say, *My God, My King.*

When I Consider How My Light Is Spent

JOHN MILTON
(1608–1674)

Milton lost his sight while still in his forties, and this sonnet bears eloquent witness to his ultimate acceptance of this burden. He continued to write great works of literature by dictation for many years.

—∿—

When I consider how my light is spent
    Ere half my days in this dark world and wide,
    And that one talent which is death to hide
    Lodg'd with me useless, though my soul more bent
To serve therewith my Maker, and present
    My true account, lest he returning chide,
    "Doth God exact day-labor, light denied?"
    I fondly ask. But Patience, to prevent
That murmur, soon replies: "God doth not need
    Either man's work or his own gifts: who best
    Bear his mild yoke, they serve him best. His state
Is kingly; thousands at his bidding speed
    And post o'er land and ocean without rest:
    They also serve who only stand and wait."

From The Prologue

ANNE BRADSTREET
(1612–1672)

A Puritan housewife, Bradstreet was the first American woman to win international acclaim as a writer. This poem seems to confer precedence to men in all things, but a contemporary reader may sense a certain irony in Bradstreet's defense of women poets.

—⟋⟍—

I am obnoxious to each carping tongue
Who says my hand a needle better fits.
A poet's pen all scorn I should thus wrong;
For such despite they cast on female wits,
If what I do prove well, it won't advance—
They'll say it's stolen, or else it was by chance.

But sure the antique Greeks were far more mild,
Else of our sex why feignéd they those Nine,
and Poesy made Calliope's own child?
So 'mongst the rest they placed the Arts Divine.
But this weak knot they will full soon untie—
The Greeks did nought but play the fools and lie.

Let Greeks be Greeks, and women what they are.
Men have precedency, and still excel.
It is but vain unjustly to wage war.
Men can do best, and women know it well.

And oh, ye high flown quills that soar the skies,
And ever with your prey still catch your praise,
If e'er you deign these lowly lines your eyes,
Give thyme or parsley wreath; I ask no bays.
This mean and unrefinéd ore of mine
Will make your glistering gold but more to shine.

To Althea, from Prison

RICHARD LOVELACE
(1618–1657)

*Lovelace was a royalist during the English Civil War, and was briefly
imprisoned by order of Parliament. It was then that he wrote this
graceful lyric, honoring his love and his loyalty to his king.*

When Love with unconfined wings
    Hovers within my gates,
And my divine Althea brings
    To whisper at the grates;
When I lie tangled in her hair,
    And fetter'd to her eye,
The gods, that wanton in the air,
    Know no such liberty.

When flowing cups run swiftly round
    With no allaying Thames,
Our careless heads with roses bound,
    Our hearts with loyal flames;
When thirsty grief in wine we steep,
    When healths and draughts go free,
Fishes, that tipple in the deep,
    Know no such liberty.

When (like committed linnets) I
    With shriller throat shall sing
The sweetness, mercy, majesty,
    And glories of my king;
When I shall voice aloud how good
    He is, how great should be,
Enlarged winds, that curl the flood,
    Know no such liberty.

Stone walls do not a prison make,
    Nor iron bars a cage;
Minds innocent and quiet take
    That for an hermitage;
If I have freedom in my love,
Angels alone that soar above,
    Enjoy such liberty.

To His Coy Mistress

ANDREW MARVELL
(1621–1678)

Marvell's famous poem of seduction is also a meditation on the fragility of human existence and a celebration of the joys of living. It's interesting to contrast its themes and images with Catullus' "Song to Lesbia" on p. 6, and Shakespeare's sonnet on p. 20.

Had we but world enough, and time,
This coyness, lady, were no crime.
We would sit down and think which way
To walk, and pass our long love's day;
Thou by the Indian Ganges' side
Shouldst rubies find; I by the tide
Of Humber would complain. I would
Love you ten years before the Flood;
And you should, if you please, refuse
Till the conversion of the Jews.
My vegetable love should grow
Vaster than empires, and more slow.
An hundred years should go to praise
Thine eyes, and on thy forehead gaze;
Two hundred to adore each breast,
But thirty thousand to the rest;
An age at least to every part,
And the last age should show your heart.
For, lady, you deserve this state,
Nor would I love at lower rate.

But at my back I always hear
Time's winged chariot hurrying near;
And yonder all before us lie
Deserts of vast eternity.

Thy beauty shall no more be found,
Nor, in thy marble vault, shall sound
My echoing song; then worms shall try
That long preserv'd virginity,
And your quaint honor turn to dust,
And into ashes all my lust.
The grave's a fine and private place,
But none, I think, do there embrace.
Now therefore, while the youthful hue
Sits on thy skin like morning glow,
And while thy willing soul transpires
At every pore with instant fires,
Now let us sport us while we may,
And now, like amorous birds of prey,
Rather at once our time devour
Than languish in his slow-chapped power.
Let us roll all our strength and all
Our sweetness up into one ball,
And tear our pleasures with rough strife
Through the iron gates of life:
Thus, though we cannot make our sun
Stand still, yet we will make him run.

An Old Pond

MATSUO BASHŌ
(1644–1694)

Bashō's poem, often offered as the quintessential example of haiku, crystallizes a moment in time just after a frog has jumped into the water.

—ᴡᴠ—

Old pond—
A frog leaps in—
Water's sound.

Epigram: Engraved on the Collar of a Dog Which I Gave to His Royal Highness

ALEXANDER POPE
(1688–1744)

Pope's famously sardonic wit was never so evident as in this brief but pointed verse.

—ɯ—

I am his Highness' dog at Kew;
Pray tell me, sir, whose dog are you?

Elegy Written in a Country Churchyard

THOMAS GRAY
(1716–1771)

*One of the most quoted of all English poems, Gray's elegy links the
lives of all of humanity in language that exquisitely balances sound,
image, and meaning.*

—m—

The curfew tolls the knell of parting day,
    The lowing herd wind slowly o'er the lea,
The plowman homeward plods his weary way,
    And leaves the world to darkness and to me.

Now fades the glimm'ring landscape on the sight,
    And all the air a solemn stillness holds,
Save where the beetle wheels his droning flight,
    And drowsy tinklings lull the distant folds;

Save that from yonder ivy-mantled tow'r
    The moping owl does to the moon complain
Of such, as wand'ring near her secret bow'r,
    Molest her ancient solitary reign.

Beneath those rugged elms, that yew-tree's shade,
    Where heaves the turf in many a mould'ring heap,
Each in his narrow cell for ever laid,
    The rude forefathers of the hamlet sleep.

The breezy call of incense-breathing Morn,
    The swallow twitt'ring from the straw-built shed,
The cock's shrill clarion, or the echoing horn,
    No more shall rouse them from their lowly bed.

For them no more the blazing hearth shall burn,
    Or busy housewife ply her evening care:
No children run to lisp their sire's return,
    Or climb his knees the envied kiss to share.

Oft did the harvest to their sickle yield,
    Their furrow oft the stubborn glebe has broke;
How jocund did they drive their team afield!
    How bow'd the woods beneath their sturdy stroke!

Let not Ambition mock their useful toil,
    Their homely joys, and destiny obscure;
Nor Grandeur hear with a disdainful smile
    The short and simple annals of the poor.

The boast of heraldry, the pomp of pow'r,
    And all that beauty, all that wealth e'er gave,
Awaits alike th' inevitable hour.
    The paths of glory lead but to the grave.

Nor you, ye proud, impute to these the fault,
    If Mem'ry o'er their tomb no trophies raise,
Where thro' the long-drawn aisle and fretted vault
    The pealing anthem swells the note of praise.

Can storied urn or animated bust
    Back to its mansion call the fleeting breath?
Can Honour's voice provoke the silent dust,
    Or Flatt'ry soothe the dull cold ear of Death?

Perhaps in this neglected spot is laid
    Some heart once pregnant with celestial fire;
Hands, that the rod of empire might have sway'd,
    Or wak'd to ecstasy the living lyre.

But Knowledge to their eyes her ample page
    Rich with the spoils of time did ne'er unroll;
Chill Penury repress'd their noble rage,
    And froze the genial current of the soul.

Full many a gem of purest ray serene,
    The dark unfathom'd caves of ocean bear:
Full many a flow'r is born to blush unseen,
    And waste its sweetness on the desert air.

Some village-Hampden, that with dauntless breast
    The little tyrant of his fields withstood;
Some mute inglorious Milton here may rest,
    Some Cromwell guiltless of his country's blood.

Th' applause of list'ning senates to command,
    The threats of pain and ruin to despise,
To scatter plenty o'er a smiling land,
    And read their hist'ry in a nation's eyes,

Their lot forbade: nor circumscrib'd alone
    Their growing virtues, but their crimes confin'd;
Forbade to wade through slaughter to a throne,
    And shut the gates of mercy on mankind,

The struggling pangs of conscious truth to hide,
    To quench the blushes of ingenuous shame,
Or heap the shrine of Luxury and Pride
    With incense kindled at the Muse's flame.

Far from the madding crowd's ignoble strife,
    Their sober wishes never learn'd to stray;
Along the cool sequester'd vale of life
    They kept the noiseless tenor of their way.

Yet ev'n these bones from insult to protect,
　　Some frail memorial still erected nigh,
With uncouth rhymes and shapeless sculpture deck'd,
　　Implores the passing tribute of a sigh.

Their name, their years, spelt by th' unletter'd muse,
　　The place of fame and elegy supply:
And many a holy text around she strews,
　　That teach the rustic moralist to die.

For who to dumb Forgetfulness a prey,
　　This pleasing anxious being e'er resign'd,
Left the warm precincts of the cheerful day,
　　Nor cast one longing, ling'ring look behind?

On some fond breast the parting soul relies,
　　Some pious drops the closing eye requires;
Ev'n from the tomb the voice of Nature cries,
　　Ev'n in our ashes live their wonted fires.

For thee, who mindful of th' unhonour'd Dead
　　Dost in these lines their artless tale relate;
If chance, by lonely contemplation led,
　　Some kindred spirit shall inquire thy fate,

Haply some hoary-headed swain may say,
　　"Oft have we seen him at the peep of dawn
Brushing with hasty steps the dews away
　　To meet the sun upon the upland lawn.

"There at the foot of yonder nodding beech
　　That wreathes its old fantastic roots so high,
His listless length at noontide would he stretch,
　　And pore upon the brook that babbles by.

"Hard by yon wood, now smiling as in scorn,
　　Mutt'ring his wayward fancies he would rove,
Now drooping, woeful wan, like one forlorn,
　　Or craz'd with care, or cross'd in hopeless love.

"One morn I miss'd him on the custom'd hill,
　　Along the heath and near his fav'rite tree;
Another came; nor yet beside the rill,
　　Nor up the lawn, nor at the wood was he;

"The next with dirges due in sad array
　　Slow thro' the church-way path we saw him borne.
Approach and read (for thou canst read) the lay,
　　Grav'd on the stone beneath yon aged thorn."

The EPITAPH

Here rests his head upon the lap of Earth
　　A youth to Fortune and to Fame unknown.
Fair Science frown'd not on his humble birth,
　　And Melancholy mark'd him for her own.

Large was his bounty, and his soul sincere,
　　Heav'n did a recompense as largely send:
He gave to Mis'ry all he had, a tear,
　　He gain'd from Heav'n ('twas all he wish'd) a friend.

No farther seek his merits to disclose,
　　Or draw his frailties from their dread abode,
(There they alike in trembling hope repose)
　　The bosom of his Father and his God.

To Jeoffry His Cat

CHRISTOPHER SMART
(1722–1771)

Smart was a religious mystic whose versification was clearly inspired by the King James version of the Bible and somewhat anticipates Blake, Whitman, and Ginsberg.

For I will consider my Cat Jeoffry.
For he is the servant of the Living God duly and daily
      serving him.
For at the first glance of the glory of God in the East he
      worships in his way.
For this is done by wreathing his body seven times round
      with elegant quickness.
For then he leaps up to catch the musk, which is the
      blessing of God upon his prayer.
For he rolls upon prank to work it in.
For having done duty and received blessing he begins to
      consider himself.
For this he performs in ten degrees.
For first he looks upon his forepaws to see if they are
      clean.
For secondly he kicks up behind to clear away there.
For thirdly he works it upon stretch with the forepaws
      extended.
For fourthly he sharpens his paws by wood.
For fifthly he washes himself.
For sixthly he rolls upon wash.
For seventhly he fleas himself, that he may not be
      interrupted upon the beat.
For eighthly he rubs himself against a post.
For ninthly he looks up for his instructions.

For tenthly he goes in quest of food.

For having consider'd God and himself he will consider his
neighbor.

For if he meets another cat he will kiss her in kindness.

For when he takes his prey he plays with it to give it a
chance.

For one mouse in seven escapes by his dallying.

For when his day's work is done his business more
properly begins.

For he keeps the Lord's watch in the night against the
adversary.

For he counteracts the powers of darkness by his electrical
skin and glaring eyes.

For he counteracts the Devil, who is death, by brisking
about the life.

For in his morning orisons he loves the sun and the sun
loves him.

For he is of the tribe of Tiger.

For the Cherub Cat is a term of the Angel Tiger.

For he has the subtlety and hissing of a serpent, which in
goodness he suppresses.

For he will not do destruction, if he is well-fed, neither will
he spit without provocation.

For he purrs in thankfulness, when God tells him he's a
good Cat.

Amazing Grace

JOHN NEWTON
(1725–1807)

Written by the former captain of a slave ship turned evangelical minister, the hymn now universally known as "Amazing Grace" (from its opening words) is sung to a melody that probably originated with African-American slaves.

—⚬—

Amazing grace! how sweet the sound
    That saved a wretch like me!
I once was lost, but now am found,
    Was blind, but now I see.

'Twas grace that taught my heart to fear,
    And grace my fears relieved;
How precious did that grace appear
    The hour I first believed.

Through many dangers, toils, and snares
    I have already come;
'Tis grace hath brought me safe thus far,
    And grace will lead me home.

The Lord has promised good to me,
    His word my hope secures;
He will my shield and portion be
    As long as life endures.

Tyger! Tyger!

WILLIAM BLAKE
(1757–1827)

This poem has often been taken as an attack on the soullessness of the Industrial Revolution, but it carries a deeper resonance as a mystical parable of the dark side of human nature.

Tyger! Tyger! burning bright
In the forests of the night,
What immortal hand or eye
Could frame thy fearful symmetry?

In what distant deeps or skies
Burnt the fire of thine eyes?
On what wings dare he aspire?
What the hand dare seize the fire?

And what shoulder, and what art,
Could twist the sinews of thy heart?
And when thy heart began to beat,
What dread hand? and what dread feet?

What the hammer? what the chain?
In what furnace was thy brain?
What the anvil? what dread grasp
Dare its deadly terrors clasp?

When the stars threw down their spears,
And watered heaven with their tears,
Did he smile his work to see?
Did he who made the Lamb make thee?

Tyger! Tyger! burning bright
In the forests of the night,
What immortal hand or eye
Dare frame thy fearful symmetry?

To a Mouse

ROBERT BURNS
(1759–1796)

Although Burns wrote in Scottish dialect, the wit and warm humanity of his verse has insured its enduring popularity for over two centuries.

—⁂—

Wee, sleeket, cowran, tim'rous beastie,
   O, what panic's in thy breastie!
Thou need na start awa sae hasty,
   Wi' bickering brattle!
I wad be laith to rin an' chase thee,
   Wi' murd'ring pattle!

   I'm truly sorry Man's dominion
Has broken Nature's social union,
   An' justifies that ill opinion,
   Which makes thee startle,
At me, thy poor, earth-born companion,
   An' fellow-mortal!

I doubt na, whyles, but thou may thieve;
What then? poor beastie, thou maun live!
   A daimen-icker in a thrave
     'S a sma' request:
I'll get a blessin wi' the lave,
   An' never miss't!

   Thy wee-bit housie, too, in ruin!
It's silly wa's the win's are strewin!
An' naething, now, to big a new ane,
   O' foggage green!

An' bleak December's winds ensuin,
          Baith snell an' keen!

Thou saw the fields laid bare an' wast,
          An' weary Winter comin fast,
          An' cozie here, beneath the blast,
                    Thou thought to dwell,
          Till crash! the cruel coulter past
                    Out thro' thy cell.

That wee-bit heap o' leaves an' stibble,
          Has cost thee monie a weary nibble!
Now thou's turn'd out, for a' thy trouble,
          But house or hald.
To thole the Winter's sleety dribble,
          An' cranreuch cauld!

          But Mousie, thou are no thy-lane,
          In proving foresight may be vain:
The best laid schemes o' Mice an' Men,
                    Gang aft agley,
An' lea'e us nought but grief an' pain,
                    For promis'd joy!

Still, thou art blest, compar'd wi' me!
          The present only toucheth thee:
But Och! I backward cast my e'e,
                    On prospects drear!
          An' forward, tho' I canna see,
                    I guess an' fear!

Ode to Joy

FRIEDRICH VON SCHILLER
(1759–1805)

This stirring expression of Romanticism by one of Germany's greatest literary figures provides the lyrics for the final movement of Beethoven's Ninth Symphony.

—⁓—

O friends, no more these sounds!
Let us sing more cheerful songs,
More full of joy!

Joy, bright spark of divinity,
Daughter of Elysium,
Fire-inspired we tread
Thy sanctuary
Thy magic power re-united
All that custom has divided
All men become brothers
Under the sway of thy gentle wings.

Whoever has created
An abiding friendship,
Or has won
A true and loving wife,
All who can call at least one soul theirs,
Join in our song of praise;
But any who cannot must creep tearfully
Away from our circle.

All creatures drink of joy
At nature's breast.
Just and unjust
Alike taste of her gift;

She gave us kisses and the fruit of the vine,
A tried friend to the end.
Even the worm can feel contentment,
And the cherub stands before God!

Gladly, like the heavenly bodies
Which He set on their courses
Through the splendor of the firmament;
Thus, brothers, you should run your race,
As a hero going to conquest.

You millions, I embrace you.
This kiss is for all the world!
Brothers, above the starry canopy
There must dwell a loving Father.
Do you fall in worship, you millions?
World, do you know your Creator?
Seek Him in the heavens;
Above the stars must He dwell.

Don't Kill that Fly!

KOBAYASHI ISSA
(1763–1827)

Issa's haiku are notable for their sympathetic treatment of everyday objects.

—⁓—

Look, don't kill that fly!
It is making a prayer to you
By rubbing its hands and feet.